AF482697

Emilio Aguinaldo

True Version of the Philippine Revolution

e-artnow 2024

Emilio Aguinaldo

True Version of the Philippine Revolution

e-artnow, 2024
Contact: eartnow.info@gmail.com

ISBN: 978-80-273-8862-2

Contents

To All Civilized Nations and Especially to the Great North American Republic

I dedicate to you this modest work with a view to informing you respecting the international events which have occurred during the past three years and are still going on in the Philippines, in order that you may be fully acquainted with the facts and be thereby placed in a position to pronounce judgment upon the issue and be satisfied and assured of the Justice which forms the basis and is in fact the foundation of our Cause. I place the simple truth respectfully before and dedicate it to you as an act of homage and as testimony of my admiration for and recognition of the wide knowledge, the brilliant achievements and the great power of other nations, whom I salute, in the name the Philippine nation, with every effusion of my soul.

The Author.

The Revolution of 1896

Spain maintained control of the Philippine Islands for more than three centuries and a half, during which period the tyranny, misconduct and abuses of the Friars and the Civil and Military Administration exhausted the patience of the natives and caused them to make a desperate effort to shake off the unbearable galling yoke on the 26th and 31st August, 1896, then commencing the revolution in the provinces of Manila and Cavite.

On these memorable days the people of Balintawak, Santa Mesa, Kalookan, Kawit, Noveleta and San Francisco de Malabon rose against the Spaniards and proclaimed the Independence of the Philippines, and in the course of the next five days these uprisings were followed by the inhabitants of the other towns in Cavite province joining in the revolt against the Spanish Government although there was no previous arrangement looking to a general revolt. The latter were undoubtedly moved to action by the noble example of the former.

With regard to the rising in the province of Cavite it should be stated that although a call to arms bearing the signatures of Don Augustin Rieta, Don Candido Firona and myself, who were Lieutenants of the Revolutionary Forces, was circulated there was no certainty about the orders being obeyed, or even received by the people, for it happened that one copy of the orders fell into the hands of a Spaniard named Don Fernando Parga, Military Governor of the province, who at that time was exercising the functions of Civil Governor, who promptly reported its contents to the Captain-General of the Philippines, Don Ramon Blanco y Erenas. The latter at once issued orders for the Spanish troops to attack the revolutionary forces.

It would appear beyond doubt that One whom eye of man hath not seen in his wisdom and mercy ordained that the emancipation of the oppressed people of the Philippines should be undertaken at this time, for otherwise it is inexplicable how men armed only with sticks and *gulok*1 wholly unorganized and undisciplined, could defeat the Spanish Regulars in severe engagements at Bakoor, Imus and Noveleta and, in addition to making many of them prisoners, captured a large quantity of arms and ammunition. It was owing to this astonishing success of the revolutionary troops that General Blanco quickly concluded to endeavour, to maintain Spanish control by the adoption of a conciliatory policy under the pretext that thereby he could quel the rebellion, his first act being a declaration to the effect that it was not the purpose of his Government to oppress the people and he had no desire "to slaughter the Filipinos.".

The Government of Madrid disapproved of General Blanco's new policy and speedily appointed Lieutenant-General Don Camilo Polavieja to supersede him, and despatched forthwith a large number of Regulars to the Philippines.

General Polavieja advanced against the revolutionary forces with 16,000 men armed with Mausers, and one field battery. He had scarcely reconquered half of Cavite province when he resigned, owing to bad health. That was in April, 1897.

Polavieja was succeeded by the veteran General Don Fernando Primo de Rivera, who had seen much active service. As soon as Rivera had taken over command of the Forces he personally led his army in the assault upon and pursuit of the revolutionary forces, and so firmly, as well as humanely, was the campaign conducted that he soon reconquered the whole of Cavite province and drove the insurgents into the mountains.

Then I established my headquarters in the wild and unexplored mountain fastness of Biak-na-bató, where I formed the Republican Government of the Philippines at the end of May, 1897.

---

1 A kind of sword —*Translator*.

The Treaty of Biak-na-bató

Don Pedro Alejandro Paterno (who was appointed by the Spanish Governor-General sole mediator in the discussion of the terms of peace) visited Biak-na-bató several times to negotiate terms of the Treaty, which, after negotiations extending over five months, and careful consideration had been given to each clause, was finally completed and signed on the 14th December, 1897, the following being the principal conditions: —

(1) That I would, and any of my associates who desired to go with me, be free to live in any foreign country. Having fixed upon Hongkong as my place of residence, it was agreed that payment of the indemnity of $800,000 (Mexican) should be made in three installments, namely, $400,000 when all the arms in Biak-na-bató were delivered to the Spanish authorities; $200,000 when the arms surrendered amounted to eight hundred stand; the final payment to be made when one thousand stand of arms shall have been handed over to the authorities and the *Te Deum* sung in the Cathedral in Manila as thanksgiving for the restoration of peace. The latter part of February was fixed as the limit of time wherein the surrender of arms should be completed.

(2) The whole of the money was to be paid to me personally, leaving the disposal of the money to my discretion and knowledge of the understanding with my associates and other insurgents.

(3) Prior to evacuating Biak-na-bató the remainder of the insurgent forces under Captain-General Primo de Rivera should send to Biak-na-bató two General of the Spanish Army to be held as hostages by my associates who remained there until I and a few of my compatriots arrived in Hongkong and the first installment of the money payment (namely, four hundred thousand dollars) was paid to me.

(4) It was also agreed that the religious corporations in the Philippines be expelled and an autonomous system of government, political and administrative, be established, though by special request of General Primo de Rivera these conditions were not insisted on in the drawing up of the Treaty, the General contending that such concessions would subject the Spanish Government to severe criticism and even ridicule.

General Primo de Rivera paid the first installment of $400,000 while the two Generals were hold as hostages in Biak-na-bató.

We, the revolutionaries, discharged our obligation to surrender our arms, which were over 1,000 stand, as everybody knows, it having been published in the Manila newspapers. But the Captain General Primo de Rivera failed to fulfill the agreement as faithfully as we did. The other installments were never paid; the Friars were neither restricted in their acts of tyranny and oppression nor were any steps taken to expel them or secularize the religious Orders; the reforms demanded were not inaugurated, though the *Te Deum* was sung. This failure of the Spanish authorities to abide by the terms of the Treaty caused me and my companions much unhappiness, which quickly changed to exasperation when I received a letter from Lieutenant-Colonel Don Miguel Primo de Rivera (nephew and private Secretary of the above-named General) informing me that I and my companions could never return to Manila.

Was the procedure of this special representative of Spain just?

Negotiations

But I and my companions were not to be kept long in our distress, grieving over the bad faith of the Spaniards, for in the month of March of the year referred to (1898) some people came to me and in the name of the Commander of the U.S.S. *Petrel* asked for a conference in compliance with the wishes of Admiral Dewey.

I had some interviews with the above-mentioned Commander, *i.e.*, during the evening of the 16th March and 6th April, during which the Commander urged me to return to the Philippines to renew hostilities against the Spaniards with the object of gaining our independence, and he assured me of the assistance of the United States in the event of war between the United States and Spain.

I then asked the Commander of the *Petrel* what the United States could concede to the Filipinos. In reply he said: "*The United States is a great and rich nation and needs no colonies.*"

In view of this reply I suggested to the Commander the advisability of stating in writing what would be agreed to by the United States, and be replied that he would refer the matter to Admiral Dewey.

In the midst of my negotiations with the Commander of the *Petrel* I was interrupted by letters from Isabelo Artacho and his solicitors, on the 5th April, claiming $200,000 of the money received from the Spanish authorities, and asserting that he (Artacho) should receive this sum as salary due to him while acting as Secretary of the Interior, he having been, it was alleged, a member of the Filipino Government established in Biak-na-bató. These letters contained the threat that failure to comply with the demand of Artacho would result in him bringing me before the Courts of Law in Hongkong. It may make the matter clearer if I mention at this point that Isabelo Artacho arrived at Biak-na-bató and made himself known to and mixed with the officers in the revolutionary camp on the 21st day of September, 1897, and was appointed Secretary of the Interior in the early part of November of that year, when the Treaty of Peace proposed and negotiated by Don Pedro Alejandro Paterno was almost concluded, as is proved by the fact that the document was signed on the 14th of December of that year.

In the light of these facts the unjust and unreasonable nature of the claim of Artacho is easily discernable, for it is monstrous to claim $200,000 for services rendered to the Revolutionary Government during such a brief period.

Moreover, it is a fact that it was agreed between ourselves (the leaders of the Revolution assembled in Biak-na-bató) that in the event of the Spaniards failing to comply with each and every one of the terms and conditions of the Agreement the money obtained from the Spanish Government should not be divided, but must be employed in the purchase of arms and ammunition to renew the war of independence.

It is therefore evident that Artacho, in making this preposterous demand, was acting as a spy for the enemy, as an agent of General Primo de Rivera, for he wanted to extinguish the rebellion by depriving its organizers and leaders of the most indispensable element, the "sinews of war," which is money. This was the view, too, of the whole of my colleagues, and it was resolved by us that I should leave Hongkong immediately and thereby avoid the litigation which Artacho seemed bent upon and thereby afford my companions time and opportunity to remove this new and wholly unexpected barrier to the realization of our cherished plans for the emancipation of our beloved fatherland. I am profoundly pleased to say that they succeeded, Artacho withdrawing the suit through a transaction.

In accordance with the decision of the meeting above referred to, I left Hongkong quietly on the 7th April, 1898, on board the steamship *Taisany*, and after calling at Saigon I reached Singapore as a passenger by the s.s. *Eridan*, landing there as secretly as possible on the 21st April. I at once proceeded to the residence of one of my countrymen.

Thus is explained the cause of the interruption of the vitally important negotiations with Admiral Dewey, initiated by the Commander of the *Petrel*.

But "Man proposes and God disposes" is a proverb which was verified in its fullest sense on this occasion, for, notwithstanding the precautions taken in my journey to avoid identification yet at 4 o'clock in the afternoon of the day I arrived at Singapore an Englishman came to the house in which I was residing and in a cautious manner stated that the United States Consul at that port, Mr. Spencer Pratt, wished to have an interview with Don Emilio Aguinaldo. The visitor was told that in that house they did not know Aguinaldo; this being the prearranged answer for any callers.

But the Englishman returned to the house several times and persisted in saying that it was no use trying to conceal the fact of Aguinaldo's arrival for Consul Pratt had received notice from Admiral Dewey of General Aguinaldo's journey to Singapore.

In reply, the Consul said he would telegraph about this matter to Admiral Dewey, who was, he said, Commander-in-Chief of the squadron which would invade the Philippines, and who had, he also stated, full powers conferred on him by President McKinley.

Between 10 or 12 in the forenoon of the next day the conference was renewed and Mr. Pratt then informed me that the Admiral had sent him a telegram in reply to the wish I had expressed for an agreement in writing. He said the Admiral's reply was —*That the United States would at least recognize the Independence of the Philippines under the protection of the United States Navy. The Consul added that there was no necessity for entering into a formal written agreement because the word of the Admiral and of the United States Consul were in fact equivalent to the most solemn pledge that their verbal promises and assurance would be fulfilled to the letter and were not to be classed with Spanish promises or Spanish ideas of a man's word of honour. In conclusion the Consul said, "The Government of North America, is a very honest, just, and powerful government."*

Being informed of what had been said by the visitor I consented to meet Consul Pratt, and had a strictly private interview with him between 9 and 12 p.m. on 22nd April, 1898, in one of the suburbs of Singapore. As soon as Mr. Pratt met me he said that war had been formally declared by the United States against Spain the day before, *i.e.*, on the 21st April.

In the course of the interview alluded to, Consul Pratt told me that as the Spaniards had not fulfilled the promises made in the Biak-na-bató Agreement, the Filipinos had the right to continue the revolution which had been checked by the Biak-na-bató arrangement, and after urging me to resume hostilities against the Spaniards he assured me that the United States would grant much greater liberty and more material benefits to the Filipinos than the Spaniards ever promised.

I then asked the Consul what benefits the United States would confer on the Philippines, pointing out at the same time the advisability of making an agreement and setting out all the terms and conditions in black and white.

Being as anxious to be in the Philippines as Admiral Dewey and the North American Consul- to renew the struggle for our Independence —I took the opportunity afforded me by these representatives of the United States, and, placing the fullest confidence in their word of honour, I said to Mr. Pratt (in response to his persistent professions of solicitude for the welfare of my countrymen) that he could count upon me when I returned to the Philippines to raise the people as one man against the Spaniards, with the one grand object in view as above mentioned, if I could take firearms with me to distribute amongst my countrymen. I assured him that I would put forth my utmost endeavours to crush and extinguish the power of Spain in the islands and I added that if in possession of one battery of a dozen field-guns I would make the Spaniards surrender Manila in about two weeks.

The Consul said he would help me to get over to the Philippines the consignment of arms in respect of which I had made the preliminary arrangements in Hongkong, and he added that he would at once telegraph to Admiral Dewey informing him of this promise in order that the Admiral might give what assistance laid in his power to make the expedition in question a success.

On the 25th April the last conference was held in the United States Consulate at Singapore. I was invited by the Consul to meet him on this occasion and as soon as we met he said he had received a telegram from the Admiral requesting him to ask me to proceed to Hongkong by first steamer to join the Admiral who was then with his squadron in Mir's Bay; a Chinese harbour close to Hongkong. I replied to this proposal in the affirmative, and gave directions to my *aide-de-camp* to at once procure passages for myself and companions, care being taken that the tickets should bear the assumed names we had adopted on the occasion of our journey from Hongkong to Singapore, it being advisable that we should continue to travel *incognito*.

On the 26th April I called on Consul Pratt to bid him adieu on the eve of my departure from Singapore by the steamship *Malacca*. The Consul, after telling me that when I got near the port of Hongkong I would be met by the Admiral's launch and taken from the *Malacca* to the American squadron (a precaution against news of my movements becoming public property, of which I highly approved), then asked me to appoint him Representative of the Philippines in the United States, there to zealously advocate official recognition of our Independence. My answer was, that I would propose him for the position of Representative of the Philippines in the United States when the Philippine Government was properly organized, though I thought it an insignificant reward for his assistance, for, in the event of our Independence becoming *un fait accompli* I intended to offer him a high position in the Customs Department, besides granting certain commercial advantages and contributing towards the cost of the war whatever sum he might consider due to his Government; because the Filipinos had already decided such a policy was the natural outcome of the exigencies of the situation and could be construed only as a right and proper token of the nation's gratitude.

But to continue the statement of facts respecting my return to Hongkong from Singapore: I left Singapore with my A.D. Cs., Sres Pilar and Leyba, bound for Hongkong by the s.s. *Malacca*, arriving at Hongkong at 2 a.m. on the 1st May, without seeing or hearing anything of the launch which I had been led by Consul Pratt to expect to meet me near the entrance of Hongkong harbour. In response to an invitation from Mr. Rounsevelle Wildman, United States Consul at Hongkong, I wended my way to the United States Consulate and between 9 and 11 p.m. of the same day I had an interview with him. Mr. Wildman told me that Admiral Dewey left for Manila hurriedly in accordance with imperative orders from his Government directing him to attack the Spanish Fleet. He was therefore unable to await my arrival before weighing anchor and going forth to give battle to the Spaniards. Mr. Wildman added that Admiral Dewey left word with him that he would send a gunboat to take me across to the Philippines. In the course of this interview with Mr. Wildman I spoke to him about the shipment of arms to the islands which I had previously planned with him, and it was then agreed among ourselves that he (Mr. Rounsevelle Wildman) and the Filipino Mr. Teodoro Sandico should complete the arrangements for the despatch of the expedition, and I there and then handed to and deposited with them the sum of $50,000.

A steam launch was quickly purchased for $15,000, while a contract was made and entered into for the purchase of 2,000 rifles at $7 each and 200,000 rounds of ammunition at $33 and 56/100 per 1000.

A week later (7th May) the American despatch-boat *McCulloch* arrived from Manila bringing news of Admiral Dewey's victory over the Spanish fleet, but did not bring orders to convey me to Manila. At 9 o'clock that night I had another interview with Consul Wildman, at his request.

On the 15th of the same month the *McCulloch* again arrived at Hongkong from Manila, this time bringing orders to convey me and my companions to Manila. I was promptly notified of this by Consul Wildman who requested that we go on board the *McCulloch* at 10 o'clock at night on 16th May. Accompanied by Consul Wildman, the Captain of the *McCulloch*, and Mr. John Barrett (who then usually styled himself "ex-Secretary of the United States Legation in Siam") we boarded an American steam launch and proceeded to Chinese Kowloon Bay, where the *McCulloch* was anchored. While bidding us adieu Mr. Barrett said he would call on me in the Philippines, which he did later on in Cavite and Malolos.

Mr. Wildman strongly advised me to establish a Dictatorship as soon as I arrived in the Philippines, and he assured me that he would use his best endeavours to have the arms already contracted for delivered to me in the Philippines, which he in fact did. [It is to be observed, though, that the first expedition having been conducted satisfactorily, the arms reaching me in due course, I was naturally grateful and had confidence in the sincerity and good faith of Consul Wildman, and there was nothing surprising therefore in the fact that I asked him to fit out another expedition and caused the sum of $67,000 to be deposited with him for that purpose. I regret to state, however, that Mr. Wildman has failed to comply with my request and I am informed that he refuses to refund the money.]

The *McCulloch* left Hongkong at 11 a.m. on the 17th May and arrived off Cavite (Manila Bay) between noon and 1 p.m. on the 19th idem. No sooner had the *McCulloch* dropped anchor than the Admiral's launch, carrying his Adjutant and Private Secretary, came alongside to convey me the flagship *Olympia*, where I was received with my Adjutant (Sr. Leyba) with the honours due to a General.

The Admiral ushered me into his private quarters, and after the exchange of the usual greetings I asked *whether it was true that he had sent all the telegrams to the Consul at Singapore, Mr. Pratt, which that gentleman had told me he received in regard to myself. The Admiral replied in the affirmative, adding that the United States had come to the Philippines to protect the natives and free them from the yoke of Spain. He said, moreover, that America is exceedingly well off as regards territory, revenue, and resources and therefore needs no colonies,* assuring me finally that *there was no occasion for me to entertain any doubts whatever about the recognition of the Independence of the Philippines by the United States.* Then Admiral Dewey asked me if I could induce the people to rise against the Spaniards and make a short, sharp, and decisive campaign of it.

I said in reply that events would speak for themselves, but while a certain arms expedition (respecting which Consul Wildman was duly informed that it would be despatched from a Chinese port) was delayed in China we could do nothing, because without arms every victory would assuredly cost us the lives of many brave and dashing Filipino warriors. The Admiral thereupon offered to despatch a steamer to hurry up the expedition. (This, be it borne in mind, in addition to the General orders he had given the Consul to assist us to procure arms and ammunition.) Then he at once placed at my disposal all the guns seized onboard the Spanish warships as well as 62 Mausers and a good many rounds of ammunition which had been brought up from Corregidor Island by the U.S.S. *Petrel*.

I then availed myself of an early opportunity to express to the Admiral my deep gratitude for the assistance rendered to the people of the Philippines by the United States, as well as my unbounded admiration of the grandeur and beneficence of the American people. I also candidly informed the Admiral that before I left Hongkong the Filipinos residing in that colony hold a meeting at which the following question was fully discussed, namely, *the possibility that after the Spaniards were defeated, and their power and prestige in the islands destroyed, the Filipinos might have to wage war against the United States owing to the American Government declining to recognize our independence. In that event the Americans, it was generally agreed, would be sure to defeat us for they would find us worn out and short of ammunition owing to our struggle with the Spaniards. I concluded by asking the gallant Admiral to excuse me for an amount of frankness that night appear to border on impudence, and assured him of the fact that I was actuated only by a desire to have a perfectly clear understanding in the interest of both parties.*

The Admiral said he was very glad to have this evidence of our earnestness and straightforwardness and he thought the Filipinos and Americans should act towards one another as friends and allies, and therefore it was right and proper that all doubts should be expressed frankly in order that explanations be made, difficulties avoided, and distrust removed; adding that, as he had already indicated, the United States would unquestionably recognize the Independence of the people of the Philippines, guaranteed as it was by the word of honour of Americans, *which, he said, is more positive, more irrevocable than any written agreement, which might not be regarded as binding when there is an intention or desire to repudiate it, as was the case in respect of the compact made with the Spaniards at Biak-na-bató. Then the Admiral advised me to at once have made a Filipino National Flag, which he said he would recognize and protect in the presence of the other nations represented by the various squadrons anchored in Manila Bay, adding, however, that he thought it advisable that we should destroy the power of Spain before hoisting our national flag, in order that the act would appear more important and creditable in the eyes of the world and of the United States in particular. Then when the Filipino vessels passed to and fro with the national flag fluttering in the breeze they would attract more attention and be more likely to induce respect for the national colours.*

I again thanked the Admiral for his good advice and generous offers, giving him to understand clearly that I was willing to sacrifice my own life if he would be thereby more exalted in the estimation of the United States, more honoured by his fellow-countrymen.

I added that under the present conditions of hearty co-operation, good fellowship and a clear understanding the whole nation would respond to the call to arms to shake off the yoke of Spain and obtain their freedom by destroying the power of Spain in all parts of the archipelago. If, however, all did not at once join in the movement that should not cause surprise, for there would be many unable to assist owing to lack of arms and ammunition, while others, again, might be reluctant to take an active part in the campaign on account of the loss and inconvenience to themselves and families that would result, from open hostility to the Spaniards.

Thus ended my first interview with Admiral Dewey, to whom I signified my intention to reside for a while at the headquarters of the Naval Commandant of Cavite Arsenal.

The Revolution of 1898

I returned to the *McCulloch* to give directions for the landing of the luggage and *war materials* which I brought over with me from Hongkong. On my way to the *McCulloch* I met several of my old associates in the 1896 revolution who had come over from Bataan province. To these friends I gave two letters directing the people of that province and Zambales to rise against the Spaniards and vigorously attack them.

Before returning to the Arsenal and when near the landing place I came across several *bancas* [large open boats] loaded with revolutionists of Kawit (my birth-place) who told me they had been looking out for me for about two weeks, the Americans having announced that I would soon return to the islands. The feeling of joy which I experienced on the occasion of this reunion with my own kith and kin-people who had stood shoulder to shoulder with me in the desperate struggles of the 1896-97 revolution-is simply indescribable. Words fail to express my feelings-joy mingled with sadness and strong determination to accomplish the salvation, the emancipation, of my beloved countrymen. Hardly had I set foot in the Naval Headquarters at Cavite, at 4 o'clock in the afternoon, than I availed myself of the opportunity to give these faithful adherents orders similar to those despatched to Bataan and Zambales.

I was engaged the whole of that night with my companions drawing up orders and circulars for the above mentioned purpose.

We were also kept very busy replying to letters which were pouring in from all sides asking for news respecting the reported return of myself to the islands and requesting definite instructions regarding a renewal of hostilities against the Spaniards.

That the invisible, albeit irresistible, hand of Providence was guiding every movement and beneficently favouring all efforts to rid the country of the detestable foreign yoke is fairly evidenced by the rapid sequence of events above recorded, for in no other way can one account for the wonderful celebrity with which news of my projected return spread far and wide.

Sixty-two Volunteers, organized and armed by the Spaniards with Mausers and Remingtons, from San Roque and Caridad, placed themselves under my orders. At first the Americans apprehended some danger from the presence of this armed force, which was promptly placed on guard at the entrance to the Arsenal. When I heard of this I went down and gave them orders to occupy Dalajican, thereby preventing the Spaniards from carrying out their intention to approach Cavite by that route.

When the Americans were informed of what I had done they were reassured, and orders were given to the Captain of the *Petrel* to hand over to me the 62 rifles and ammunition which Admiral Dewey had kindly promised. About 10 a.m. the *Petrel's* launch landed the arms and ammunition in question at the Arsenal and no time was lost in distributing the arms among the men who were by this time coming in ever increasing numbers to offer their services to me and expressing their willingness to be armed and assigned for duty at the outposts and on the firing line.

During the evening of the 20th May the old Revolutionary officer Sr. Luciano San Miguel (now a General in command of a Brigade) came to me and asked for orders, which were given to him to effect the uprising of the provinces of Manila, Laguna, Batangas, Tayabas, Bulakan, Morong, Pampanga, Tarlak, Newva Ecija and other northern provinces. He left the same night to execute the orders.

During the 21st, 22nd and 23rd and subsequent days of that month my headquarters were simply besieged by my countrymen, who poured into Cavite from all sides to offer their services in the impending struggle with the Spaniards. To such an extent, indeed, were my quarters in the Arsenal invaded that I soon found it necessary to repair to another house in the town, leaving the place entirely at the disposal of the U.S. Marines, who were then in charge of and guarding Cavite Arsenal.

The Dictatorial Government

On the 24th May a Dictatorial Government was established, my first proclamation being issued that day announcing the system of government then adopted and stating that I had assumed the duties and responsibilities of head of such government. Several copies of this proclamation were delivered to Admiral Dewey and through the favour of his good offices forwarded to the representatives of the Foreign Powers then residing in Manila, notwithstanding our lack of intercourse with Manila.

A few days later the Dictatorial Government was removed to the house formerly occupied by the Spanish Civil Governor of Cavite, because, owing to the great number of visitors from the provinces and the rapid increase of work the accommodation in the private house was wholly inadequate and too cramped. It was while quartered in the first mentioned house that glad tidings reached me of the arrival at Cavite of the long-expected arms expedition. The whole cargo, consisting of 1,999 rifles and 200,000 rounds of ammunition, besides other special munitions of war, was landed at the very same dock of the Arsenal, and was witnessed by the U.S.S. "*Petrel.*"

I immediately despatched a Commission to convey to the Admiral my thanks for the trouble he had taken in sending to hurry up the expedition. I also caused my Commissioners to inform the Admiral that I had fixed the 31st May as the day when the Revolutionary Forces should make a General attack upon the Spaniards. The Admiral returned the compliment by sending his Secretary to congratulate me and my Government upon the activity and enthusiasm displayed in preparing for the campaign, but he suggested that it was advisable to postpone the opening of the campaign to a later date in order that the insurgent troops might be better organized and better drilled. I replied to the Admiral through his Secretary that there was no cause for any anxiety for everything would be in perfect readiness by the 31st and, moreover, that the Filipinos were very anxious to free themselves from the galling Spanish yoke, that they would therefore fight and my troops would make up for any deficiency in discipline by a display of fearlessness and determination to defeat the common enemy which would go far to ensure success, I was, I added, nevertheless profoundly grateful to the Admiral for his friendly advice.

I promptly gave orders for the distribution of the arms which had just arrived, sending some to various provinces and reserving the remainder for the revolutionaries of Kawit, the latter being smuggled into the district of Alapang during the night of 27th May.

The First Triumphs

The next day (8th May, 1898), just when we were distributing arms to the revolutionists of Kawit, in the above mentioned district a column, composed of over 270 Spanish Naval Infantry, appeared in sight. They were sent out by the Spanish General, Sr. Peña, for the purpose of seizing the said consignment of arms.

Then it was that the first engagement of the Revolution of 1898 (which may be rightly styled a continuation of the campaign of 1896-97) took place. The battle raged from 10 a.m. to 3 p.m., when the Spaniards ran out of ammunition and surrendered, with all their arms, to the Filipino Revolutionists, who took their prisoners to Cavite. In commemoration of this glorious achievement I hoisted our national flag in presence of a great crowd, who greeted it with tremendous applause and loud, spontaneous and prolonged cheers for "Independent Philippines" and for "the generous nation" —the United States of America. Several officers and Marines from the American fleet who witnessed the ceremony evinced sympathy with the Filipino cause by joining in the natural and popular rejoicings of the people.

This glorious triumph was merely the prelude to a succession of brilliant victories, and when the 31st May came-the date fixed for general uprising of the whole of the Philippines-the people rose as one man to crush the power of Spain.

The second triumph was effected in Binakayan, at a place known as *Polvorin*, where the Spanish garrison consisting of about 250 men was attacked by our raw levvies and surrendered in a few hours, their stock of ammunition being completely exhausted.

I again availed myself of the opportunity to hoist our national flag and did so from an upper story of the *Polvorin* facing the sea, with the object of causing the sacred insignia of our Liberty and Independence to be seen fluttering in the breeze by the warships, representing all the great and civilized nations of the world, which were congregated in the harbour observing the providential evolution going on in the Philippines after upwards of three hundred years of Spanish domination.

Scarcely had another hour elapsed before another flag was seen flying over the steeple of the Church at Bakoor-which is also in full view of vessels in the harbour-being the signal of another triumph of our troops over the Spanish forces which held that town. The garrison consisted of about 300 men, who surrendered to the Revolutionary Army when their ammunition was exhausted.

And so the Revolution progressed, triumph following triumph in quick succession, evidencing the power, resolution and ability of the inhabitants of the Philippines to rid themselves of any foreign yoke and exist as an independent State, as I affirmed to Admiral Dewey and in respect of which he and several American Commanders and officers warmly congratulated me, specially mentioning the undeniable triumphs of the Philippine Army as demonstrated and proved by the great number of prisoners we brought into Cavite from all parts of Luzon.

The Philippine Flag

In conformity with my orders issued on the 1st of September, all Philippine vessels hoisted the national flag, the Marines of the Filipino flotilla being the first to execute that order. Our little flotilla consisted of some eight Spanish steam launches (which had been captured) and five vessels of greater dimensions, namely, the *Taaleño, Baldyan, Taal, Bulucan,* and *Purisima Concepcion.* These vessels were presented to the Philippine Government by their native owners and were converted by us, at our Arsenal, into gunboats, 8 and 9 centimetre guns, taken from the *sunken Spanish warships*, being mounted on board.

Ah! what a beautiful, inspiring joyous sight that flag was fluttering in the breeze from the topmasts of our vessels, side by side, as it were, with the ensigns of other and greater nations, among whose mighty warships our little cruisers passed to and fro dipping their colours, the ensign of Liberty and Independence! With what reverence and adoration it was viewed as it suddenly rose in its stately loneliness crowning our victories, and, as it were, smiling approvingly upon the undisciplined Philippine Army in the moment of its triumphs over the regular forces of the Spanish Government! One's heart swells and throbs again with the emotions of extreme delight; the soul is filled with pride, and the goal of patriotism seems well-nigh reached in the midst of such a magnificent spectacle!

At the end of June I called on Admiral Dewey, who, after complimenting me on *the rapid triumphs of the Philippine Revolution*, told me he had been asked by the German and French Admirals why he allowed the Filipinos to display on their vessels a flag that was not recognized. Admiral Dewey said his reply to the French and German Admirals was-with *his knowledge and consent the Filipinos used that flag*, and, apart from this, he was of opinion that in view of the courage and steadfastness of purpose displayed in the war against the Spaniards the Filipinos deserved the right to use their flag.

I thereupon expressed to the Admiral my unbounded gratitude for such unequivocal protection, and on returning to the shore immediately ordered the Philippine flotilla to convey troops to the other provinces of Luzon and to the Southern islands, to wage war against the Spaniards who garrisoned them.

Expedition to Bisayas

The expedition to Bisayas was a complete success as far as the conveyance of our troops to the chief strategic points was concerned, our steamers returning safely to Cavite after landing the soldiers. The steamer *Bulusan*, however, which sailed for Masbate with Colonel Sr. Mariano Riego de Dios' column destined for duty in Samar was sighted by the Spanish gunboats *Elcano* and *Uranus*, which gave chase, and the former proving the faster overtook and attacked the *Bulusan* doing so much damage to her that she foundered after a hot engagement in which considerable damage was done to the Spaniard. Happily the crew and troops on board of the *Bulusan* saved their lives by swimming ashore.

The Steamer "Compania de Filipinas"

In a few days the Spanish steamer *Compania de Filipinas* was brought to Cavite by my countrymen, who captured her in the harbour of Aparri. Cannon were at once mounted on board this vessel and she was loaded with troops and despatched for Olongapo, but she had not gone far before I sent another gunboat to recall her because Admiral Dewey requested me to do so in order that a question raised by the French Consul might be duly settled. The Admiral having been informed that when captured the *Compania de Filipinas* was flying the Spanish flag abstained from interfering in the matter and handed the French Consul's protest over to me, affirming at the same time that *he and his forces were in no way concerned in the matter*.

This incident, which was soon settled, clearly demonstrates the recognition of and protection extended to the Philippine Revolution by Admiral Dewey.

The *Filipinas* (as this steamer has since been styled) was again despatched to Olongapo and on her way back landed troops in the provinces of Cagayan and the Batanes islands for the purpose of wresting the government of those districts from Spain. This steamer, whose name has more recently been changed to *Luzon*, is at present ashore in the Rio Grande, in Cagayan, where she was beached owing to some damage to her machinery.

When our steamers were leaving the harbour with troops for the provinces they dipped their ensigns in passing Admiral Dewey's flagship *Olympia*, performing this act in conformity with the rules of international courtesy, a demonstration of friendship that was invariably promptly responded to in the usual way.

The Proclamation of Independence

The Dictatorial Government decided that the proclamation of Independence should take place on the 12th June, the ceremony in connection therewith to be held in the town of Kawit. With this object in view I sent a Commission to inform the Admiral of the arrangement and invite him to be present on the occasion of the formal proclamation of Independence, a ceremony which was solemnly and impressively conducted. The Admiral sent his Secretary to excuse him from taking part in the proceedings, stating the day fixed for the ceremony was mail day.

About the end of that month (June) the Spanish gunboat *Leyte* escaped from the Macabebe river and reached Manila Bay, where she was seized by General Torres' troops. She had on board part of the troops and volunteers which were under the command of the Filipino Colonel Sr. Eugenio Blanco, but on being sighted by an American gunboat she voluntarily surrendered. Admiral Dewey delivered to me all the prisoners and arms on board the vessel, which latter, however, he took possession of; but after the fall of Manila he demanded that I should give back the prisoners to him.

On the 4th July the first United States military expedition arrived, under command of General Anderson, and it was quartered in Cavite Arsenal. This distinguished General called on me in the Filipino Government House at Cavite, an honour and courtesy which I promptly returned, as was right and proper, seeing that we were friends, of equal rank, and allies. In the course of official intercourse General Anderson solemnly and completely endorsed the promises made by Admiral Dewey to me, asserting on his word of honour that America had not come to the Philippines to wage war against the natives nor to conquer and retain territory, but only to liberate the people from the oppression of the Spanish Government.

A few days before the arrival of this military expedition, and others that followed under command of General Merritt, Admiral Dewey sent his Secretary to my Government to ask me to grant permission for the stationing of American troops in Tambo and Maytubig, Paranaque and Pasay. In view of the important promises of Admiral Dewey, above mentioned, the Dictatorial Government consented to the movement of troops as proposed.

During that month (July) Admiral Dewey accompanied by General Anderson visited Cavite, and after the usual exchange of courtesies he said —"You have had ocular demonstration and confirmation of all I have told you and promised you. How pretty your flag is! It has a triangle, and is something like the Cubans'. Will you give me one as a memento when I go back home?"

I replied that I was fully satisfied with his word of honour and of the needlessness of having our agreement in documentary form. As to the flag he wanted, he could have one whenever he wished.

The Admiral continued: *Documents are useless when there is no sense of honour on one side, as was the case in respect of the compact with the Spaniards, who failed to act up to what had been written and signed. Have faith in my word, and I assure you that the United States will recognize the independence of the country. But I recommend you to keep a good deal of what we have said and agreed secret at present. I further request you to have patience if any of our soldiers insult any Filipinos, for being Volunteers they are as yet undisciplined.*

I replied that I would bear in mind all his advice regarding cautiousness, and that with respect to the misconduct of the soldiers orders had already been issued enjoining forbearance, and I passed the same remarks to the Admiral about unpleasantness possibly arising through lack of discipline of our own forces.

The Spanish Commission

At this juncture the Admiral suddenly changed the topic of conversation and asked —"Why don't the people in Manila rise against the Spaniards as their countrymen in the provinces have done? Is it true that they accept the *autonomy* offered by General Augustin with a representative Assembly? Is the report which has reached me true, that a Filipino Commission has been sent from Manila to propose to you the acceptance of that *autonomy* coupled with a recognition of your rank of General, as well as recognition of the rank held by your companions?"

"The people of Manila," I answered, "are quiet because they have no arms and because as merchants and landlords they fear that their valuable properties and money in the banks will be confiscated by the Spaniards if they rise up and begin burning and destroying the property of others. On this account they had ostensibly accepted *autonomy*, not because that was what they wanted but more as a means of deceiving the Spaniards and being allowed to live in peace; but I am confident that all the Filipinos in Manila are for *independence*, as will be proved the very day our troops capture Manila. At that time I fully expect the people of Manila will join with us in raising loud cheers for the Independence of the Philippines, making fresh demonstrations of loyalty to our Government."

I also told him it was true that a Mixed Commission had arrived and in the name of General Augustin and Archbishop Nozaleda made certain proposals; but they made known to us their intention to adhere to our Cause. The members of the Commission said the Spaniards instructed them to say they came *motu propio*1 without being formally appointed or 'coached' by the Spanish authorities in what they should say, representing, on the contrary, that they were faithful interpreters of the sentiment of the people of Manila and that they had good reason for believing that if I was willing to accept *autonomy* General Augustin and Archbishop Nozaleda would recognize my rank of General, and that of my companions, would give me the $1,000,000 indemnity agreed upon at Biak-na-bató and still unpaid, as well as liberal rewards for and salaries to the members of a popular Assembly promises which the Commissioners did not put any faith in, though some of them held the opinion that the money should be accepted because it would reduce the funds of the Spanish Government and also because the money had been wrung from Filipinos. The Commissioners, I added, left after assuring me that the people in Manila would rise against the Spaniards if supplied with arms, and that the best thing I could do was to make an attack on Manila at the places they pointed out as being the weakest parts of the Spanish defense and consequently the easiest to overcome.

I thanked the Commission for their loyalty and straightforwardness, told them they would be given an escort to take them safely back to the Spanish lines, and that when they got back they should inform those who had sent them that they were not received because they were not duly accredited and that even if they had brought credentials according to what they had seen and heard from the Revolutionists Don Emilio Aguinaldo would certainly not consider, much less accept, their proposals respecting autonomy because the Filipino people had sufficient experience to govern themselves, that they are tired of being victimised and subjected to gross abuses by a foreign nation under whose domination they have no wish to continue to live, but rather wish for their *independence*. Therefore the Spaniards might prepare to defend their sovereignty, for the Filipino Army would vigorously assault the city and with unflagging zeal prosecute the siege until Manila was captured.

I also told the Commissioners to tell Archbishop Nozaleda that he was abusing the privileges and authority of his exalted position; that such conduct was at variance with the precepts of His Holiness the Pope, and if he failed to rectify matters I would throw light on the subject in a way which would bring shame and disgrace upon him. I added that I knew he and General Augustin had commissioned four Germans and five Frenchmen to disguise themselves and assassinate me in the vain hope that once I am disposed of the people of the Philippines would calmly submit to the sovereignty of Spain, which was a great mistake, for were I assassinated, the inhabitants of the Philippines would assuredly continue the struggle with greater vigor than ever. Other men would come forward to avenge my death. Lastly I recommended the Commissioners to tell the people in Manila to go on with their trades and industries and be perfectly at ease about our Government, whose actions were guided in the paths of rectitude and justice, and that since there were no more Friars to corrupt the civic virtues, the Filipino Government was now endeavouring to demonstrate its honesty of purpose before the whole world. There was therefore no reason why they should not go on with their business as usual and should not think of leaving Manila and coming into the Camp, where the resources were limited, where already more were employed than was necessary to meet the requirements of the Government and the Army, and where, too, the lack of arms was sorely felt.

The Commissioners asked me what conditions the United States would impose and what benefits they would confer on the Filipinos, to which I replied that is was difficult to answer that question in view of the secret I was in honour bound to keep in respect of the terms of the Agreement, contenting myself by saying that they could learn a good deal by carefully observing the acts, equivalent to the exercise of sovereign rights, of the Dictatorial Government, and especially the occular demonstrations of such rights on the waters of the harbour.

These statements, which were translated by my interpreter, Sr. Leyba, made such an impression on the Admiral that he interrupted, asking —"Why did you reveal our secret?" Do you mean that you do not intend to keep inviolate our well understood silence and watchword?

I said in reply that I had revealed nothing of the secret connected with him and the Consul.

The Admiral then thanked me for my cautiousness, bid we good-by and left with General Anderson, after requesting me to refrain from assaulting Manila because, he said, they were studying a plan to take the Walled City with their troops, leaving the suburbs for the Filipino forces.

He advised me, nevertheless, to study other plans of taking the city in conjunction with their forces, which I agreed to do.

---

1 Of their own free will and accord —*Translator*.

More American Troops

A few days later American troops arrived, and with them came General Merritt. The Admiral's Secretary and two officers came to the Dictatoriat Government and asked that we allow them to occupy our trenches at Maytubig; from the harbour side of that place right up to the main road, where they would form a continuation of our lines at Pasay and Singalong. This I also agreed to on account of the solemn promises of the Admiral and the trust naturally placed in them owing to the assistance rendered and recognition of our independence.

Ten days after the Americans occupied the trenches at Maytubig (this move being well known by the Spaniards who were entrenched at the Magazine in San Antonio Abad) their outposts, composed of a few men only, were surprised by the Spaniards, who made a night attack on them. They had barely time to get out of their beds and fall back on the centre, abandoning their rifles and six field-guns in their precipitate retreat.

The firing being distinctly heard, our troops immediately rushed to the assistance of our friends and allies, repulsing the Spaniards and recapturing the rifles and field-guns, which I ordered to be returned to the Americans as a token of our good-will and friendship.

General Noriel was opposed to this restitution, alleging that the arms did not belong to the Americans since the Filipino troops captured them from the Spaniards. But I paid no attention to the reasonable opposition of my General and gave imperative instructions that they be returned to the Americans, showing thereby clearly and positively the good-will of the Filipinos. The said rifles and field-guns, with a large quantity of ammunition, was therefore restored to those who were then our allies, notwithstanding the fact of General Noriel's brigade capturing them at a cost of many lives of our compatriots.

Later on more American reinforcements arrived and again Admiral Dewey, through his Secretary, asked for more trenches for their troops, averring that those which we had given up to them before were insufficient. We at once agreed and their lines were then extended up to Pasay.

The Thirteenth of August

The 13th August arrived, on which day I noticed a general advance of the American land and sea forces towards Manila, the former being under command of General Anderson at Paranaque.

Subsequently I ordered a general assault of the Spanish lines and in the course of this movement General Pio del Pilar succeeded in advancing through Sampalok and attacked the Spanish troops who where defending the Puente Colgante,1 causing the enemy to fall back on the Bridge of Spain. The column commanded by our General, Sr. Gregorio II. del Pilar, took the suburbs of Pretil, Tendo, Divisoria and Paseo de Azcarraga, situated north of Manila city; while General Noriel's command, near Pasay, took the suburbs of Singalong and Pako, and following the American column he out-flanked the Spaniards who were defending San Antonio Abad. The Spanish officers observing General Noriel's move ordered their men to retreat towards the Walled City, whereupon the Americans who held the foremost trenches entered Malate and Ermita without firing a shot. At this point the Americans met General Noriel's troops who had captured the above mentioned suburbs and were quartered in the building formerly used by the Exposicion Regional de Filipinas,2 in the Normal, and in Sr. Perez' house in Paco.

In Santa Ana (the eastern section of Manila) General Ricarto successfully routed five companies of Spaniards, being aided in this by the manoeuvres of General Pio del Pilar's brigade.

---

1 Suspension bridge. —*Translator*.
2 Philippine Local Exhibition. —*Translator*.

First Clouds

Our troops saw the American forces landing on the sea shore near the Luneta and Paseo de Santa Lucia, calling the attention of everybody to the fact that the Spanish soldiers in the city forts were not firing on them (the Americans), a mystery that was cleared up at sunset when details of the capitulation of Manila, by General Jaudenes in accordance with terms of an agreement with General Merritt, became public property—a capitulation which the American Generals reserved for their own benefit and credit in contravention of the agreement arrived at with Admiral Dewey in the arrangement of plans for the final combined assault on and capture of Manila by the allied forces, American and Filipino.

Some light was thrown upon this apparently inexplicable conduct of the American Commanders by the telegrams which I received during that day from General Anderson, who wired me from Maitubig asking me to issue orders forbidding our troops to enter Manila, a request which I did not comply with because it was not in conformity with the agreement, and it was, moreover, diametrically opposed to the high ends of the Revolutionary Government, that after going to the trouble of besieging Manila for two months and a half, sacrificing thousands of lives and millions of material interests, it should be supposed such sacrifices were made with any other object in view than the capture of Manila and the Spanish garrison which stubbornly defended the city.

But General Merritt, persistent in his designs, begged me not only through the Admiral but also through Major Bell to withdraw my troops from the suburbs to (as it was argued) prevent the danger of conflict which is always to be looked for in the event of dual military occupation; also by so doing to avoid bringing ridicule upon the American forces; offering, at the same time, in three letters, to negotiate after his wishes were complied with. To this I agreed, though neither immediately nor at one time, but making our troops retire gradually up to the blockhouses in order that the whole of the inhabitants of Manila should witness the proceedings of our troops and amicability toward our American allies.

Up to that time, and in fact right up to the time when the Americans openly commenced hostilities against us, I entertained in my soul strong hopes that the American Commanders would make absolute with their Government the verbal agreement made and entered into with the Leader of the Philippine Revolution, notwithstanding the indications to the contrary which were noticeable in their conduct, especially in respect of the conduct of Admiral Dewey, who, without any reason or justification, one day in the month of October seized all our steamers and launches.

Being informed of this strange proceeding, and at the time when the Revolutionary Government had its headquarters in Malolos, I despatched a Commission to General Otis to discuss the matter with him. General Otis gave the Commissioners a letter of recommendation to the Admiral to whom he referred them; but the Admiral declined to receive the Commission notwithstanding General Otis's recommendation.

Notwithstanding the procedure of the American Commanders, so contrary to the spirit of all the compacts and antecedents above mentioned, I continued to maintain a friendly attitude towards them, sending a Commission to General Merritt to bid him farewell on the eve of his departure for Paris. In his acknowledgement of his courtesy General Merritt was good enough to say that he would advocate the Filipino Cause in the United States. In the same manner I sent to Admiral Dewey a *punal*1 in a solid silver scabbard and a walking stick of the very best cane with gold handle engraved by the most skilful silversmiths as a souvenir and mark of our friendship. This the Admiral accepted, thereby in some measure relieving my feelings and the anxiety of my compatriots constituting the Revolutionary Government, whose hearts were again filled with pleasant hopes of a complete understanding with Admiral Dewey.

----

1 Short sword —*Translator*.

Vain Hopes

Vain indeed became these hope when news arrived that Admiral Dewey had acted and was continuing to act against the Revolutionary Government by order of His Excellency Mr. McKinley, who, prompted by the "Imperialist" party, had decided to annex the Philippines, granting, in all probability, concessions to adventurers to exploit the immense natural wealth lying concealed under our virgin soil.

This news was received in the Revolutionary camp like a thunderbolt out of a clear sky. Some cursed the hour and the day we treated verbally with the Americans; some denounced the ceding of the suburbs, while others again were of opinion that a Commission should be sent to General Otis to draw from him clear and positive declarations on the situation, drawing up a treaty of amity and commerce if the United States recognize our independence or at once commence hostilities if the States refused.

In this crisis I advised moderation and prudence, for I still had confidence in the justice and rectitude of United States Congress, which, I believed, would not approve the designs of the Imperialist party and would give heed to the declarations of Admiral Dewey, who, in the capacity of an exalted Representative of the United States in these Islands concerted and covenanted with me and the people of the Philippines recognition of our independence.

In fact in no other way was such a serious matter to be regarded, for if America entrusted to Admiral Dewey the honour of her forces in such a distant region, surely the Filipinos might equally place their trust in the word of honour of such a polished, chivalrous gentleman and brave sailor, in the firm belief, of course, that the great and noble American people would neither reject his decision nor expose to ridicule the illustrious conqueror of the Spanish fleet.

In the same way the not less known and notorious circumstances, that the American Commanders who came soon after the echoes of the Admiral's victory reached their native shores, namely, Generals Merritt, Anderson and Otis, proclaimed to the people of the Philippines that America *did not come to conquer territories, but to liberate its inhabitants from the oppression of Spanish Sovereignty.* I would therefore also expose to universal ridicule and contempt the honour of these Commanders if the United States, by repudiating their official and public acts, attempts to annex these islands by conquest.

The American Commission

With such prudent as well as well founded reflections, I succeeded in calming my companions shortly before the official news arrived reporting that the Washington Government, acting on Admiral Dewey's suggestion, had intimated its intention to despatch a Civil Commission to Manila which would treat with the Filipinos with a view to arriving at a definite understanding respecting the government of the Islands.

Joy and satisfaction now filled the breasts of all the Revolutionists, and I thereupon set about the appointment of a Commission to meet the American Commissioners. At the same time I gave strict orders that the most friendly relations should be maintained with the Americans, enjoining toleration and overlooking of the abuses and atrocities of the soldiery because the effect on the Commissioners would not be good it they found us at loggerheads with their nation's forces.

But the abases of the Americans were now becoming intolerable. In the market-place at Arroceros they killed a woman and a little boy under the pretext that they were surprising a gambling den, thus causing the greatest indignation of a great concourse of people in that vicinity.

My Adjutants, too, who hold passes permitting them to enter Manila with their uniform and sidearms, were molested by being repeatedly stopped by every patrol they met, it, being perfectly evident that, the intention was to irritate them by exposing them to public ridicule.

While this sort of thing was going on as against our people the American Commanders and officers who visited our camp were treated with the utmost courtesy and consideration.

In Lacoste Street an American guard shot and killed a boy seven years of age for taking a banana from a Chinaman.

The searching of houses was carried on just as it was during the Spanish regime, while the American soldiers at the outposts often invaded our lines, thus irritating our sentries. It would make this book a very large volume if I continued to state seriatim the abuses and atrocities committed by the American soldiery in those days of general anxiety.

It seemed as if the abuses were authorised or at least winked at in official quarters for the purpose of provoking an outbreak of hostilities. Excitement ran high among all classes of people, but the Filipino Government, which had assumed responsibility for the acts of the people, by the constant issue of prudent orders succeeded in calming the excited populace and maintained peace, advising all sufferers to be patient and prudent pending the arrival of the Civil Commission.

Impolitic Acts

At such a critical juncture as this, and before the anxiously-awaited Civil Commission arrived, it occurred to General Otis, Commandant of the American forces, to commit two more impolitic acts. One of them was the order to search our telegraph offices in Sagunro Street, in Tondo, where the searching party seized the apparatus and detained the officer in charge, Sr. Reyna, in the Fuerza Santiago1 under the pretext that he was conspiring against the Americans.

How and why was Sr. Reyna conspiring? Was not this sufficient for the Filipino Government to give the order to attack and rescue Reyna and thereby we (eight thousand strong) be plunged immediately into war with the United States? Was there any reason for conspiring when the power was in our own hands? And, above all, would a telegraphist, be likely to interfere in *affaires de guerre* when there was an army near by to attend to such matters?

It was abundantly manifest that the object was by wounding the feelings of and belittling the Filipino Government to provoke a collision, and it was clear also that this system of exasperating us was not merely the wanton act of the soldiery but was actually prompted by General Otis himself, who, imbued with imperialistic tendencies, regarded the coming of the Civil Commission with disfavour and especially would it be unsatisfactory that this Commission should find the Philippines in a state of perfect tranquility, because it was evident to the said General, as well as to the whole world, that the Filipinos would assuredly have arrived at a definite amicable agreement with the aforesaid Commission if it reached the islands while peace prevailed.

We, the Filipinos, would have received the Commission with open arms and complete accord as honourable Agents of the great American nation. The Commissioners could have visited all our provinces, seeing and taking note of the complete tranquility throughout our territory. They could have seen our cultivated lands, examined our Constitution and investigated the administration of public affairs in perfect peace and safety, and have felt and enjoyed the inimitable charm of our Oriental style, —half negligent, half solicitude, warmth and chilliness, simple confidence and suspiciousness; characteristics which cause descriptions of contact with us to be depicted by foreigners in thousands of different hues.

Ah! but neither did General Otis nor the Imperialists wish for such a landscape. It was better for their criminal designs that the American Commission should view the desolation and horrors of war in the Philippines, inhaling on the very day of their arrival the revolting odour emitted from American and Filipino corpses. It was better for their purposes that that gentleman, Mr. Schurman, President of the Commission, should return from Manila, limiting his investigation to inquiries among the few Filipinos, who, seduced with gold, were siding with the Imperialists. It were better for them that the Commission should view the Philippines problem through fire and slaughter, in the midst of whizzing bullets and the uncontrolled passion of infuriated foes, thus preventing them from forming correct judgment of the exact and natural conditions of the problem. Ah! it was, lastly, better that the Commission return to the States defeated in its mission of obtaining peace and blaming me and other Filipinos for its inability to settle matters, when, in reality, I and all the Philippine people were longing that that peace had been concluded yesterday, —long before now-but an honest and honourable peace, honourable alike for the United States and the Philippine Republic in order that it be sincere and everlasting.

The second impolitic act of General Otis was the issue of a proclamation on the 4th of January, 1899, asserting in the name of President McKinley the sovereignty of America in these islands, with threats of ruin, death and desolation to all who declined to recognize it.

I, Emilio Aguinaldo-though the humble servant of all, am, as President of the Philippine Republic, charged with the safeguarding of the rights and independence of the people who appointed me to such an exalted position of trust and responsibility-mistrusted for the first time the honour of the Americans, perceiving of course that this proclamation of General Otis completely exceeded the limits of prudence and that therefore no other course was open to me but to repel with arms such unjust and unexpected procedure on the part of the commander of friendly forces.

I protested, therefore, against such a proclamation-also threatening an immediate rupture of friendly relations, —for the whole populace was claiming that an act of treason had been committed, plausibly asserting that the announcement of the Commission applied for by Admiral Dewey was a ruse, and that what General Otis was scheming for was to keep us quiet while he brought reinforcement after reinforcement from the United States for the purpose of crashing our untrained and badly equipped Army with one blow.

But now General Otis acted for the first time like a diplomatist, and wrote me, through his Secretary, Mr. Carman, a letter inviting the Filipino Government to send a Commission to meet an American Commission for the purpose of arriving at an amicable arrangement between both parties; and although I placed no trust in the professions of friendly intentions of the said General-whose determination to prevent the Commission arriving at a peaceful solution of the difficulties was already evident —I acceded to the request, partly because I saw the order, dated 9th January, given by the above mentioned General confirmed, and on the other hand to show before the whole world my manifest wishes for the conservation of peace and friendship with the United States, solemnly compacted with Admiral Dewey.

---

1 The "Black Hole" of Manila.

The Mixed Commission

Conferences of the Mixed Commission, Americans and Filipinos, were held in Manila from the 11th to the 31st of the said month of January, the Filipino Commissioners clearly expressing the wish of our people for recognition as an independent nation.

They also frankly stated the complaints of the Filipino people about the abuses and atrocities of the American soldiery, being attentively and benevolently listened to by the American Commissioners. The latter replied that they had no authority to recognize the Filipino Government, their mission being limited to hearing what the Filipinos said, to collect data to formulate the will of our people and transmit it fully and faithfully to the Government of Washington, who alone could arrive at a definite decision on the subject. These conferences ended in perfect harmony, auguring well for happier times and definite peace when Mr. McKinley should reply to General Otis's telegrams transmitting our wishes with his favourable recommendations, as the American Commissioners said.

Outbreak of Hostilities

While I, the Government, the Congress and the entire populace were awaiting the arrival of such a greatly desired reply, many fairly overflowing with pleasant thoughts, there came the fatal day of the 4th February, during the night of which day the American forces suddenly attacked all our lines, which were in fact at the time almost deserted, because being Saturday, the day before a regular feast day, our Generals and some of the most prominent officers had obtained leave to pass the Sabbath with their respective families.

General Pantaleon Garcia was the only one who at such a critical moment was at his post in Maypajo, north of Manila, Generals Noriel, Rizal and Ricarte and Colonels San Miguel, Cailles and others being away enjoying their leave.

General Otis, according to trustworthy information, telegraphed to Washington stating that the Filipinos had attacked the American Army. President McKinley read aloud the telegram in the Senate, where the Treaty of Paris of the 10th December, 1898, was being discussed with a view to its ratification, the question of annexation of the Philippines being the chief subject of debate, and through this criminal procedure secured the acceptation of the said Treaty *in toto* by a majority of only three votes,1 which were cast simultaneously with a declaration that the voters sided with the "Ayes" on account of war having broken out in these Islands.

This singular comedy could not continue for a great length of time because the Filipinos could never be the aggressors as against the American forces, with whom we had sworn eternal friendship and in whose power we expected to find the necessary protection to enable us to obtain recognition of our independence from the other Powers.

The confusion and obfuscation of the first moments was indeed great, but before long it gave place to the light of Truth which shone forth serene, bringing forth serious reflections.

When sensible people studied the acts of Mr. McKinley, sending reinforcement after reinforcement to Manila at a time after an armistice was agreed upon and even when peace with Spain prevailed; when they took into account that the despatch of the Civil Commission to settle terms of a treaty of amity with the Filipinos was being delayed; when, too, they knew of the antecedents of my alliance with Admiral Dewey, prepared and arranged by the American Consuls of Singapore and Hongkong, Mr. Pratt and Mr. Wildman; when they became acquainted with the actual state of affairs on the 4th February knowing that the Filipinos were awaiting the reply of Mr. McKinley to the telegram of General Otis in which he transmitted the peaceful wish of the Filipino people of live as an independent nation; when, lastly, they riveted their attention to the terms of the Treaty of Paris, the approval of which, in as far as it concerned the annexation of the Philippines, was greeted with manifestations of joy and satisfaction by the Imperialist party led by Mr. McKinley, then their eyes were opened to the revelations of truth, clearly perceiving the base, selfish and inhuman policy which Mr. McKinley had followed in his dealings with us the Filipinos, sacrificing remorselessly to their unbridled ambition the honour of Admiral Dewey, exposing this worthy gentleman and illustrious conqueror of the Spanish fleet to universal ridicule; for no other deduction can follow from the fact that about the middle of May of 1898, the U.S.S. *McCulloch* brought me with my revolutionary companions from Hongkong, by order of the above mentioned Admiral, while now actually the United States squadron is engaged in bombarding the towns and ports held by these revolutionists, whose objective is and always has been Liberty and Independence.

The facts as stated are of recent date and must still be fresh in the memory of all.

Those who in May, 1898, admired the courage of Admiral Dewey's sailors and the humanitarianism of this illustrious Commander in granting visible aid to an oppressed people to obtain freedom and independence, surely cannot place an honest construction upon the present inhuman war when contrasting it with those lofty and worthy sentiments.

I need not dwell on the cruelty which, from the time of the commencement of hostilities, has characterized General Otis's treatment of the Filipinos, shooting in secret many who declined to sign a petition asking for autonomy. I need not recapitulate the ruffianly abuses which the

American soldiers committed on innocent and defenseless people in Manila, shooting women and children simply because they were leaning out of windows; entering houses at midnight without the occupants' permission-forcing open trunks and wardrobes and stealing money, jewellery and all valuables they came across; breaking chairs, tables and mirrors which they could not carry away with them, because, anyhow, they are consequences of the war, though improper in the case of civilized forces. But what I would not leave unmentioned is the inhuman conduct of that General in his dealings with the Filipino Army, when, to arrange a treaty of peace with the Civil Commission, of which Mr. Schurman was President, I thrice sent emissaries asking for a cessation of hostilities.

General Otis refused the envoys' fair and reasonable request, replying that he would not stop hostilities so long as the Philippine Army declined to lay down their arms.

But why does not this Army deserve some consideration at the hands of General Otis and the American forces? Had they already forgotten the important service the Filipino Army rendered to the Americans in the late war with Spain?

Had General Otis forgotten the favours conferred on him by the Filipino Army, giving up to him and his Army the suburbs and blockhouses which at such great sacrifice to themselves the Filipinos had occupied?

Why should General Otis make such a humiliating condition a prime factor or basis of terms of peace with an Army which stood shoulder to shoulder with the American forces, freely shedding its blood, and whose heroism and courage were extolled by Admiral Dewey and other Americans?

This unexplained conduct of General Otis, so manifestly contrary to the canons of international law and military honour, is eloquent testimony of his deliberate intention to neutralize the effects of Mr. Schurman's pacific mission.

What peace can be concerted by the roaring of cannon and the whizzing of bullets?

What is and has been the course of procedure of General Brooke in Cuba? Are not the Cubans still armed, notwithstanding negotiations for the pacification and future government of that Island are still going on?

Are we, perchance, less deserving of liberty and independence than those revolutionists?

Oh, dear Philippines! Blame your wealth, your beauty for the stupendous disgrace that rests upon your faithful sons.

You have aroused the ambition of the Imperialists and Expansionists of North America and both have placed their sharp claws upon your entrails!

Loved mother, sweet mother, we are here to defend your liberty and independence to the death! We do not want war; on the contrary, we wish for peace; but honourable peace, which does not make you blush nor stain your forehead with shame and confusion. And we swear to you and promise that while America with all her power and wealth could possibly vanquish us; killing all of us; but enslave us, never!!!

No; this humiliation is not the compact I celebrated in Singapore with the American Consul Pratt. This was not the agreement stipulated for with Mr. Wildman, American Consul in Hongkong. Finally, it was not the subjection of my beloved country to a new alien yoke that Admiral Dewey promised me.

It is certain that these three have abandoned me, forgetting that I was sought for and taken from my exile and deportation; forgetting, also, that neither of these three solicited my services in behalf of American Sovereignty, they paying the expense of the Philippine Revolution for which, manifestly, they sought me and brought me back to your beloved bosom!

If there is, as I believe, one God, the root and fountain of all justice and only eternal judge of international disputes, it will not take long, dear mother, to save you from the hands, of your unjust enemies. So I trust in the honour of Admiral Dewey: So I trust in the rectitude of the great people of the United States of America, where, if there are ambitious Imperialists, there are defenders of the humane doctrines of the immortal Monroe, Franklin, and Washington;

unless the race of noble citizens, glorious founders of the present greatness of the North American Republic, have so degenerated that their benevolent influence has become subservient to the grasping ambition of the Expansionists, in which latter unfortunate circumstance would not death be preferable to bondage?

Oh, sensible American people! Deep is the admiration of all the Philippine people and of their untrained Army of the courage displayed by your Commanders and soldiers. We are weak in comparison with such Titanic instruments of your Government's ambitious Caesarian policy and find it difficult to effectively resist their courageous onslaught. Limited are our warlike resources, but we will continue this unjust, bloody, and unequal struggle, not for the love of war-which we abhor-but to defend our incontrovertible rights of Liberty and Independence (so dearly won in war with Spain) and our territory which is threatened by the ambitions of *a party* that is trying to subjugate us.

Distressing, indeed, is war! Its ravages cause us horror. Luckless Filipinos succumb in the confusion of combat, leaving behind them mothers, widows and children. America could put up with all the misfortunes she brings on us without discomfort; but what the North American people are not agreeable to is that she should continue sacrificing her sons, causing distress and anguish to mothers, widows and daughters to satisfy the whim of maintaining a war in contravention of their honourable traditions as enunciated by Washington and Jefferson.

Go back, therefore, North American people, to your old-time liberty. Put your hand on your heart and tell me: Would it be pleasant for you if, in the course of time, North America should find herself in the pitiful plight, of a weak and oppressed people and the Philippines, a free and powerful nation, then at war with your oppressors, asked for your aid promising to deliver you from such a weighty yoke, and after defeating her enemy with your aid she set about subjugating you, refusing the promised liberation?

Civilized nations! Honourable inhabitants of the United States, to whose high and estimable consideration I submit this unpretentious work, herein you have the providential facts which led to the unjust attack upon the existence of the Philippine Republic and the existence of those for whom, though unworthy, God made me the principal guardian.

The veracity of these facts rests upon my word as President of this Republic and on the honour of the whole population of eight million souls, who, for more than three hundred years have been sacrificing the lives and wealth of their brave sons to obtain due recognition of the natural rights of mankind-liberty and independence.

If you will do me the honour to receive and read this work and then pass judgment impartially solemnly declaring on which side right and justice rests, your respectful servant will be eternally grateful.

(Signed) Emilio Aguinaldo. *Tarlak, 23rd September, 1899.*

---

1 Many of the American papers reported that the majority was *one* vote only in excess of the absolutely requisite two-thirds majority.